▲ *East side of the castle with Kempenich and Rodendorf Houses*

Eltz Castle (a »**Ganerbenburg**«). Truces regulated the peaceful communal life of the joint heirs, their rights and duties, and the administration and upkeep of the castle. The oldest preserved agreement of this kind dates back to 1323. A »Ganerbe« (old German »ganarpeo«) was a joint heir or member of a community of heirs. These heirs lived together on a divided estate but communal housekeeping was not the rule.

In the 14th century, Elector *Balduin of Trier*, from the House of Luxembourg and an uncle of Charles IV, tried to enforce the peace in his electorate with its centres Trier, Koblenz and Boppard. The free knights of the Holy Roman Empire objected to the Elector's policy. They thought it limited their right to private warfare. Thus, on June 15, 1331, the knights of the castles of Waldeck, Schöneck, Ehrenburg (all from the Hunsrück district) and Eltz formed an offensive and defensive alliance. They undertook to provide a total of 50 heavily armed horsemen as well as their castle garrisons to fight the Elector. In the same year Balduin began to suppress the knights' alliance. He erected a siege tower on a rock in front of Eltz Castle. The rectangular, two-storeyed tower, the **Trutz- or Baldeneltz**, was typical of Balduin's smaller constructions. It had battlements, a double gate with an entrance with pointed arch and three-sided fortifications. From there catapults hurled heavy stone balls at Eltz Castle, some of which can still be seen in the inner courtyard of the castle. By cutting off the supply lines, Eltz Castle was forced to capitulate. The Hunsrück castles also capitulated as a result of similar tactics. In 1333, the Eltz family pleaded for hostilities to cease. On January 9, 1336, the »Pax de Eltz« was concluded, the Eltz feud ended and the castle remained in the hands of Elector Balduin who in 1337 made *Johann von Eltz* its Burgrave. In 1354, Emperor *Charles IV* himself gave Eltz Castle as fief to Elector Balduin and his successor *Boemund*. Thus, the free knights of Eltz became the vassals of the Elector of Trier and had to take Eltz Castle and Baldeneltz from the Elector as feudal tenure.

The Eltz feud remained the only important military conflict in the castle's history.

A period of great building activity began in the 15th century. In 1441, on the west side the Rübenach House was completed under *Lancelot* and *Wilhelm vom silbernen Löwen* (the name Eltz-Rübenach comes from the bailiwick of Rübenach near Koblenz, acquired by *Richard vom silbernen Löwen* in 1277).

The architectural variety which immediately strikes the visitor upon entering the inner courtyard is largely due to the side of the **Rübenach House** [5] facing the courtyard: the multi-cornered, half-timbered turrets, the restored, simple but stern bay resting on two basalt columns above the entrance to the house and particularly the picturesque Late Gothic chapel bay.

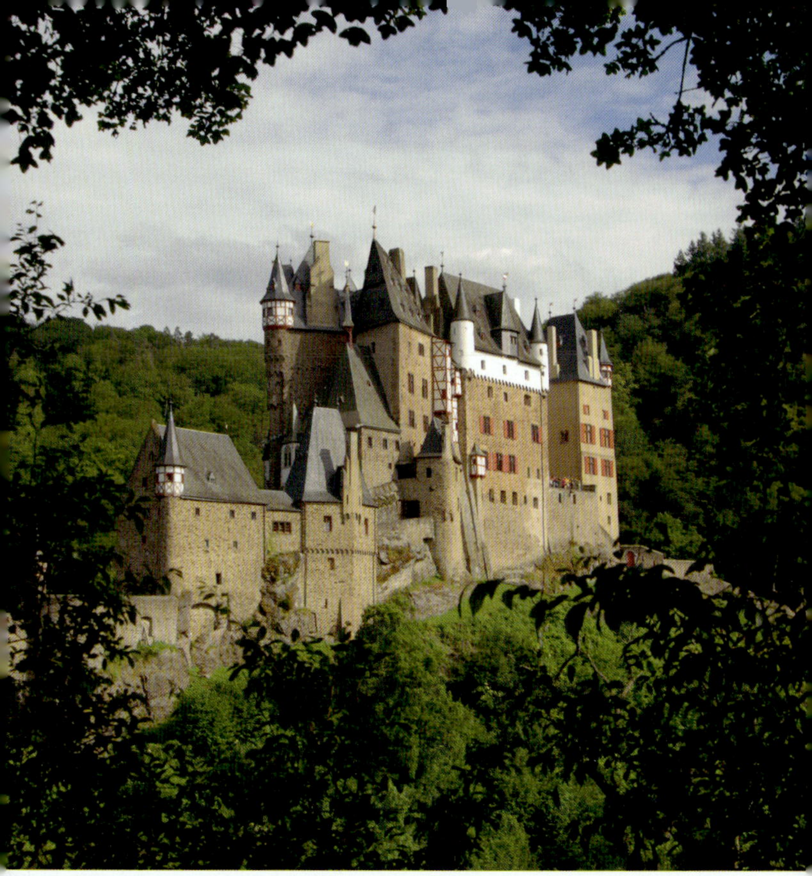

▲ *West side of the castle with the gatehouse, Rübenach House and Platt Eltz*

Around 1300 **Kleinrodendorf House** was added, in the early 16th century **Großrodendorf House** [**13–15**]. Their courtyard front has a vaulted entrance hall supported by three pillars. In the wall next to it, there is a mosaic of a Madonna dating back to the 19th century (the name Eltz-Rodendorf goes back to the marriage of *Hans Adolf* to *Katherine von Brandscheid zu Rodendorf* in 1563; thus, he acquired Rodendorf (Châteaurouge) in the Lorraine district of Bouzonville, and took on its name). When the Rodendorf Houses were finished, building began on the **Kempenich Houses** [9–12]. Their architecture and finely arranged half-timbering complete the charming overall impression of the inner courtyard. A cistern was connected to the lower end of the mighty octagonal stair tower. The cistern that supplied the castle with much of its water was once accessible from the courtyard. The main entrance of the Kempenich Houses is protected by a porch. In its upper storey there is a room with a bay which rests on two octagonal basalt pillars. The round arches between the pillars bear the inscriptions: BORGTORN ELTZ 1604 and ELTZ-MERCY, indicating the beginning of building work and the first builders of these houses. Only under *Hans Jacob von Eltz* and his wife *Anna Elizabeth von Metzenhausen* was building work stepped up and finally completed. The bosses of the porch's groin vaulting (1651) with the coats-of-arms of Eltz and Metzenhausen, as well as the splendid tuff Baroque coat-of-arms of alliance beneath the centre windows of the bay, dating back to 1661, are reminders of this. The same coats-of-arms are also found on the wrought iron window gratings of the Kempenich »Untersaal« and on the courtyard railings.

The 500-year building history harmoniously combines all styles from the Romanesque to the Early Baroque. The castle, consisting of eight towers with living quarters grouped around an inner courtyard, was representative of the so-called »Randhausburg«. Up to one hundred members of the family used to live in almost as many rooms.

The family »von und zu Eltz« did the electorates of Mainz and Trier great service. *Jacob von Eltz* (1510–1581) became one of the important electors in the history of the Archbishopric of Trier. He studied in Louvain and was, inter alia, rector of the University of Trier in 1564. He was then chosen Elector by the chapter in the Church of St Florin, Koblenz, on April 7, 1567. Unlike some of his predecessors and other church princes, Jacob had been ordained long before acceding to power. He became one of the main leader of the Counter-Reformation and considered the Jesuits his most important allies.

The House of Eltz was to hold another important position in the electorate of Trier: on June 15, 1624, *Hans Jacob von Eltz* was appointed

Inner courtyard with Kempenich Houses ▶

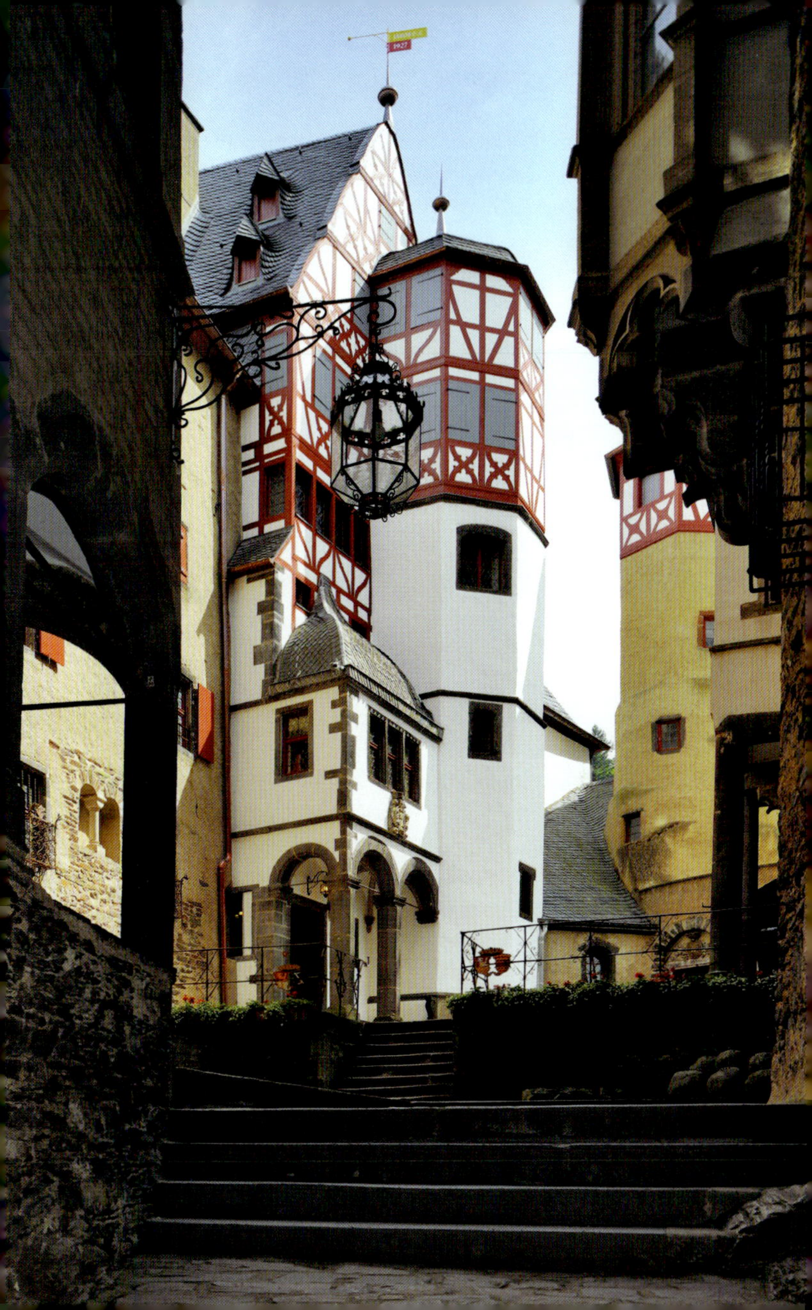

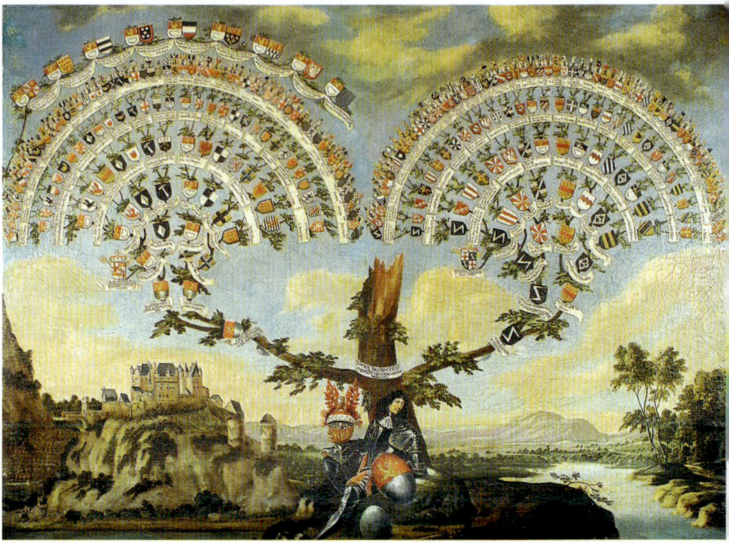

▲ *Genealogical table of the Eltz family, oil painting of 1663*

Marshal by the Elector of Trier. He thus became the leader of the knights.

The Eltz family gained power and importance not only in Trier but also in Mainz. *Philipp Karl* was unanimously chosen Elector by the Mainz chapter on June 9, 1732. Thus, he became the spiritual leader and most powerful prince of the church north of the Alps. As head of the German church, he ranked second only to the Pope. As Chancellor of the Holy Roman Empire, he presided over the Imperial Diet of Regensburg as most important person after the Emperor. Philipp Karl called the other eight electors to Frankfurt, requested them to vote and cast the ninth deciding vote himself.

The House of Eltz had extensive lands, especially in the electorates of Trier and Mainz. The Eltz estates in Koblenz, Trier, Boppard, Würzburg, Mainz and Eltville indicate where the Eltz family's main interests lay. In 1736, the family acquired Vukovar near Belgrade for 175,000 Rhenish guilders. This estate, by far the family's largest, was the main domicile of the line of Eltz vom goldenen Löwen from the mid-19th century until expulsion in 1944. Since the Second World War, the family has lived in the »Eltzer Hof« in Eltville/Rhine (this main line of the House of Eltz has also been called Eltz-Kempenich since the 16th century).

In Vienna, 1733, Emperor Charles VI conferred the title of count on the line vom goldenen Löwen for services rendered during the Reformation and the wars against the Turks. In addition, it was given the privilege of being able to create nobility in the Emperor's name, choose notaries, legitimize illegitimate children, bestow coats-of-arms with shield and crest, appoint public clerks and judges, release serfs, etc.

Eltz Castle is one of the few Rhenish castles never to have been destroyed by force. By skillful diplomacy, particularly of the only Protestant line of the House Eltz-Bliescastel-Brunswick, the castle survived the turbulence of the Thirty Years' War without being damaged. The majority of the castles on the Rhine were destroyed during the Palatinate War of Succession (1688–1689). However, as a French officer, *Johann-Anton von Eltz-Üttingen* succeeded in preventing the destruction of Eltz Castle.

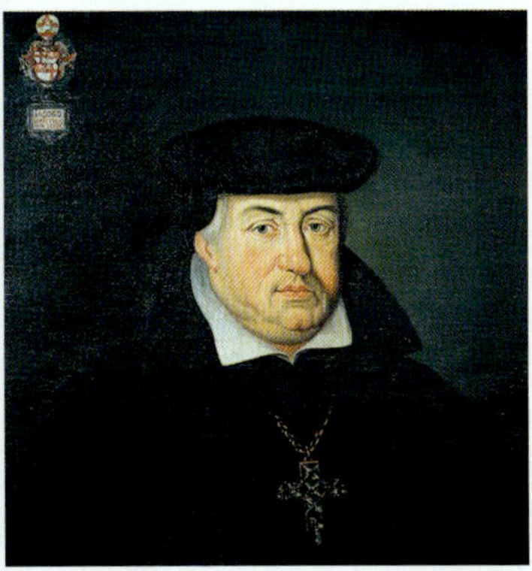

▲ *Jacob III von Eltz (1510–1581)*

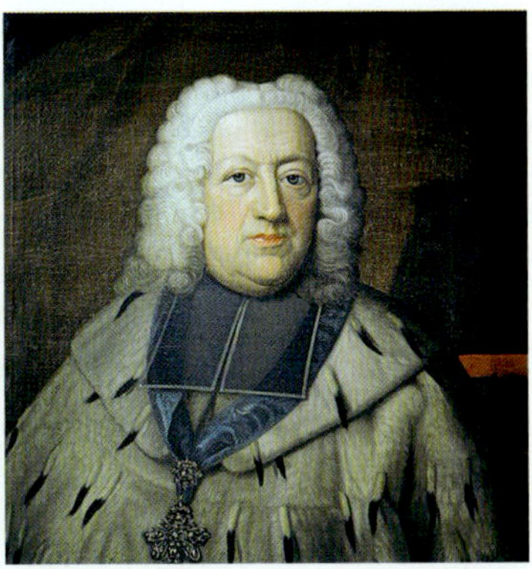

▲ *Philipp Karl von Eltz (1665–1743)*

During French rule on the Rhine (1795–1815), *Count Hugo Philipp* was treated like an emigrant and his estates on the Rhine and in the Trier area were confiscated. He was called »Bürger Graf Eltz« (Citizen Count Eltz!). Eltz Castle and its estates were subordinated to garrison headquarters in Koblenz. It later turned out that the count hat not emigrated at all but had stayed in Mainz. Thus, in 1797, the use of the estates and its revenues was returned to him. In 1815, Count Hugo Philipp became the sole owner of the castle by buying the Rübenach House and the property of the Eltz-Rübenach line; the Eltz-Rodendorf line had died out and the Eltz-Kempenich line had already inherited its property in 1786.

In the 19th century, *Count Karl* restored the ancestral castle in the course of the Romantic movement and the growing interest in the Middle Ages. Restoration work lasted from 1845 to about 1888 and cost 184,000 Marks. F. W. E. Roth was asked to write the »History of the Noblemen and Counts of Eltz«. It was published in two volumes in Mainz, 1890. Both before and after restoration was completed, important 19th century personalities visited Eltz Castle to see what Count Karl had accomplished. Amongst them were Emperor William II, the great French poet Victor Hugo and the English painter William Turner.

Eltz Castle has belonged to the Eltz family for 850 years. The present owner, Dr. Graf Karl von und zu Eltz-Kempenich, called Faust von Stromberg, lives in Eltville/Rhine where the family has had a residence since the mid-18th century. Administrators have lived in the castle since then. Depending on the period, they have had such titles as captain of the castle or castellan.

Tour of the castle

The tour begins in the **reception hall** of the Rübenach House. It only became an armoury in the 19th century, during the course of the Romantic movement. Arms were originally kept under lock and key. On the window side: full armour, breast plates, helmets, chain mail and the armour of a foot soldier with a round shield. The oldest firearms in the collection are the 15th century arquebuses. The matchlocks and

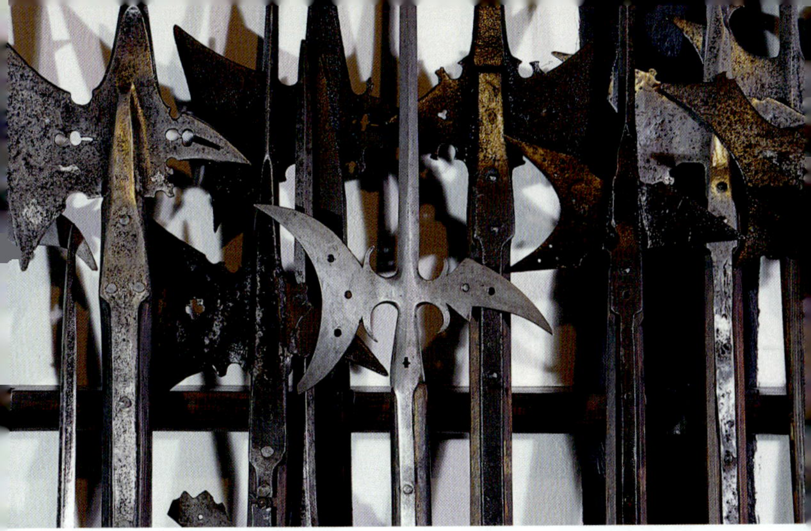

▲ *Halberds in the reception hall of the Rübenach House*

wheellocks on display were further developments of the 16th century. They were activated by cord and flint respectively. Halberds (to the left and right of the door) were the typical weapons of foot soldiers from the 14th century onwards. They consisted of battle-axe, spear or pike and a hook for unseating horsemen. The collection or Oriental weapons consists of valuable scimitars, a round shield and a variety of bows and arrows.

The adjoining room is the so-called **Rübenach Untersaal**. This is a typical late medieval living room of well-to-do castle dwellers. Its architecture is original. The room was heated by an open fire, as were about 30 of the almost 100 rooms in the castle, indicating the building's high standard of comfort. In the Middle Ages, the chest was the most common piece of furniture for storing things. It was also used for transportation purposes. The folding chair could be used when travelling. The back was pulled out and the chair simply folded together.

The Flemish **tapestries** (around 1580) are called »verdures« because of their dominant green colour. They depict some rather exotic-look-

Pages 12/13: *Eltz castle after Stanfield, around 1830* ▶▶

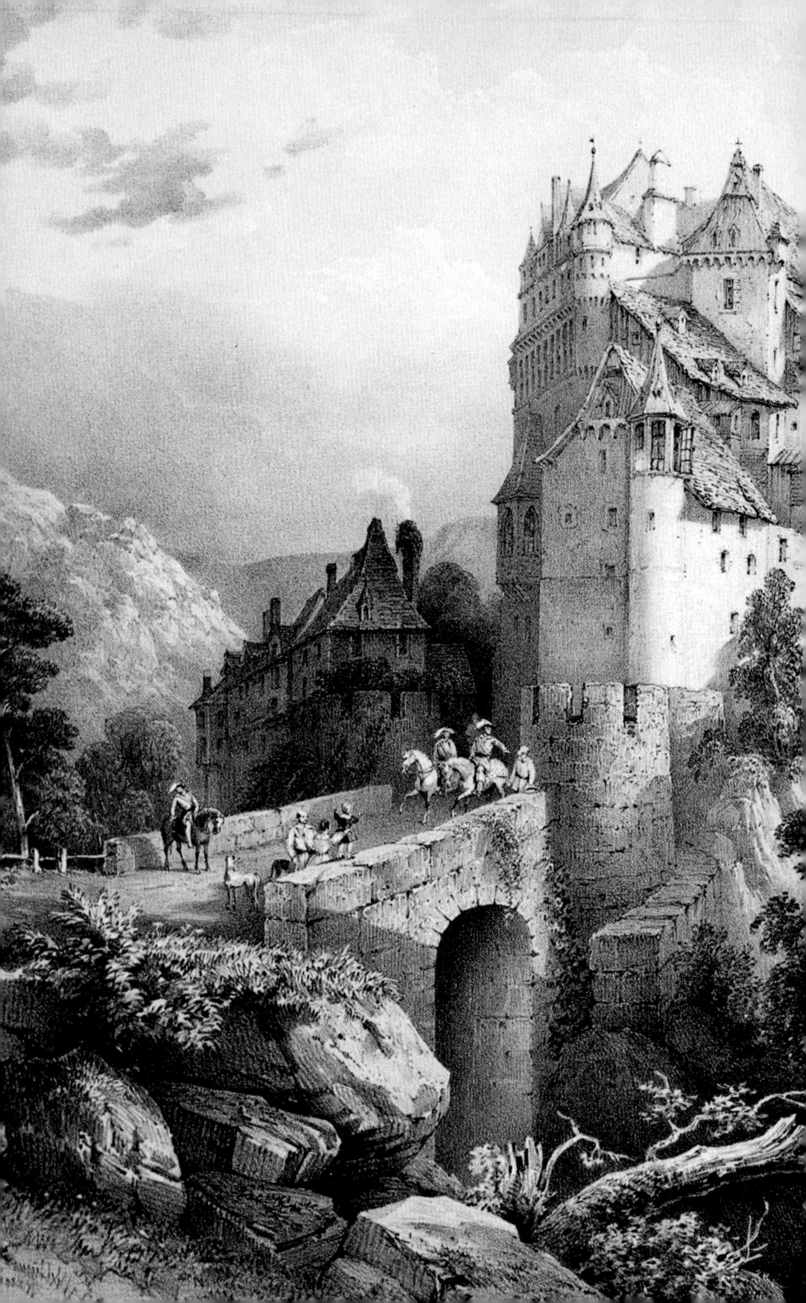

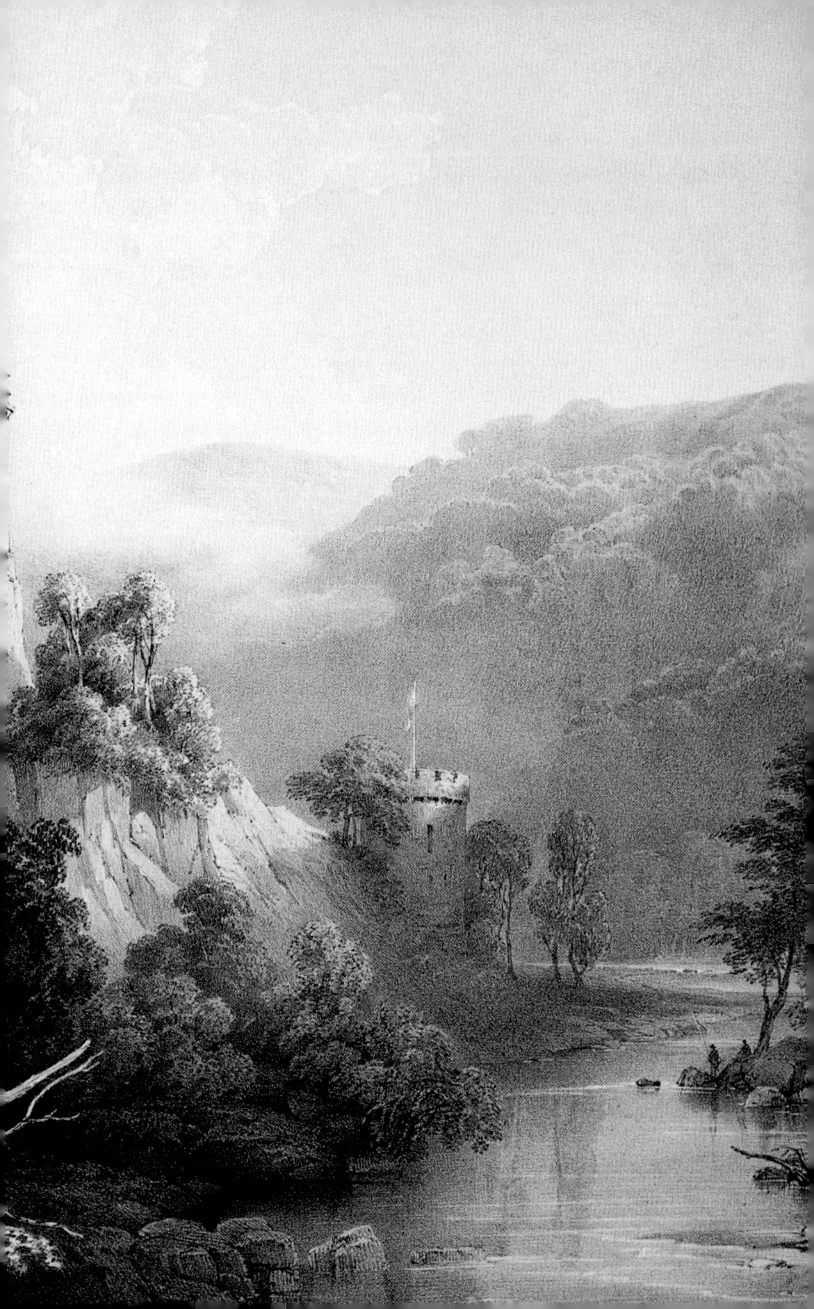

ing animals and plants. This is typical of a period in which Europeans were gradually discovering the world and wanted to record their impressions of it in pictures. The clock is South German, late 15th century, with a Late Gothic dial.

The **panel paintings** are quite remarkable: to the left on the half-timbered wall a »Gregorian Mass« (1494) from the Cologne school of painting, above the door the »Adoration of the Magi« (around 1550). *Lucas Cranach the Elder*, one of the most important German painters of the 16th century, painted the »Madonna with the Grapes«, around 1540. The »Crucifixion Scene« (1495) between the windows is also from the Cologne school of painting. On the fireplace wall, there is an »Adoration Scene« from the Cranach school and a picture which probably comes from the workshop of *Pacher*, the Southern Tyrolean painter and wood sculptor. It depicts an open bible (early 16th century).

The large **bed chamber** in the upper storey of the Rübenach House is reached by a narrow staircase. The room's flower and foliage decorations are of the 15th century origin, restored in the 19th century.

The scenes in the Late Gothic **chapel bay** begin with the Annunciation in the vault and range from the Adoration of the Magi in the stained glass windows to the Crucifixion and Descent from the Cross in the wall paintings.

The **bed** (mostly 1520) has Late Gothic folds, hunting, battle and tournament scenes on the cornice of the baldachin and ancestral coats-of-arms on the front. The bed is high in order to make the best possible use of the room's warmth. The curtains also helped to retain the heat.

The **chest on legs** (»Stollenschrank«) originates from Cologne, around 1560. One of the castle's 20 toilets is located in one of the half-timbered bays.

The adjoining rooms are a **dressing room** (on the right) with Late Gothic wall paintings (restored in the 19th century) and a **writing cabinet** (on the left) with painted decorations dating from 1882.

The first room in the **Rodendorf House** is the **Elector's room**. It was probably given this name in the 19th century when the portraits of the two electors Philipp Carl and Jakob were hung here. The furniture

Chapel bay with stained glass windows from the 15th century ▶

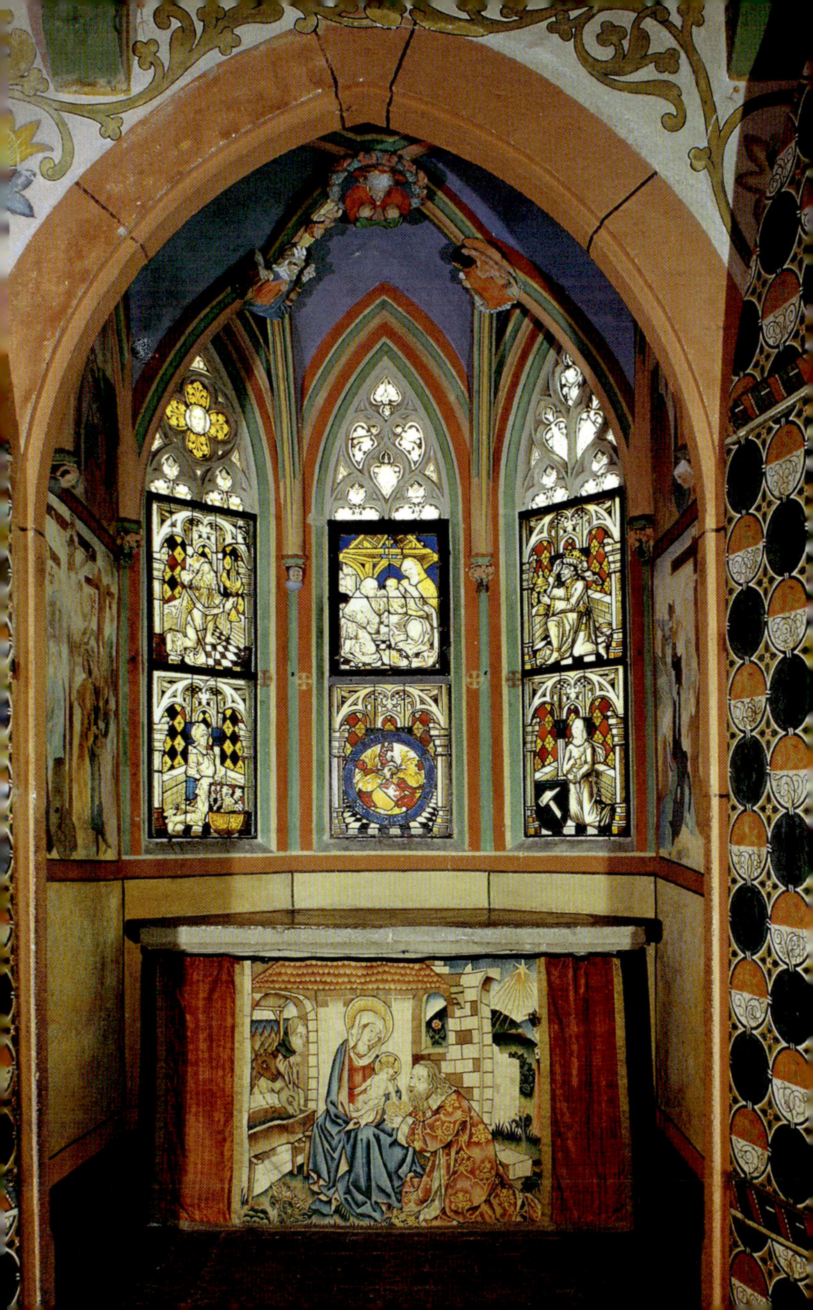

consists of a Baroque cabinet and four Rococo chairs (probably Flemish, first half of the 18th century). The room's decorative centre piece is a **tapestry** worked by the *van der Brüggen brothers* from Brussels (around 1680). It depicts the season of autumn with the start of the hunt with dogs and hunters, garlands of autumn fruit and a ram's head symbolizing fertility.

For many visitors, the **knight's hall** is the highlight of the tour. This fine hall is the largest room in the castle. It was open to all families for joint festivities. While the jester's masks below the centre beam and in some of the corners are symbols of freedom of speech, the rose of silence above the exit is a symbol of secrecy and discretion. In the cornice below the oak-beamed ceiling, the noble and mighty family of Eltz is represented in the coats-of-arms of the related aristocratic families. Coats-of-arms are distinguishing emblems borne on the knight's shield. Heraldry of this type was already developing during the first Crusades. It was customary to cover cold walls of elegant living quarters and festive halls with decorative draperies.

The **tapestry**, which was manufactured around 1700 in the Brussels area, shows the evening meal of the Greek sun god Helius with Selene, the goddess of the moon. The collection of small cannons, dating from 1730, was made on a scale of about one to six. They are extremely exact miniatures of the cannons used in the 18th century. The insides of the tubes indicate that they were also fired with live ammunition. **Maximilian's armour** (1520) is named after Emperor Maximilian, the »last German knight«. A knight in armour such as this carried a weight of up to 40 kg. The armour on both sides of the fireplace is late 16th century. There are also three **iron caskets**, dating back to the late 16th century. In the middle of each heavy lid is a lock with a key. A simple turn of the key opens seven spring bolts simultaneously.

The **Wamboldt room** on the floor below contains a richly inlaid South German cabinet (around 1600), four 17th century chairs, linen press, spinning wheel, spool and some small 16th and 17th century portraits.

The adjoining room, the so-called **Comtesse room**, is one of the castle's many living rooms. It was quite usual to render the wood-

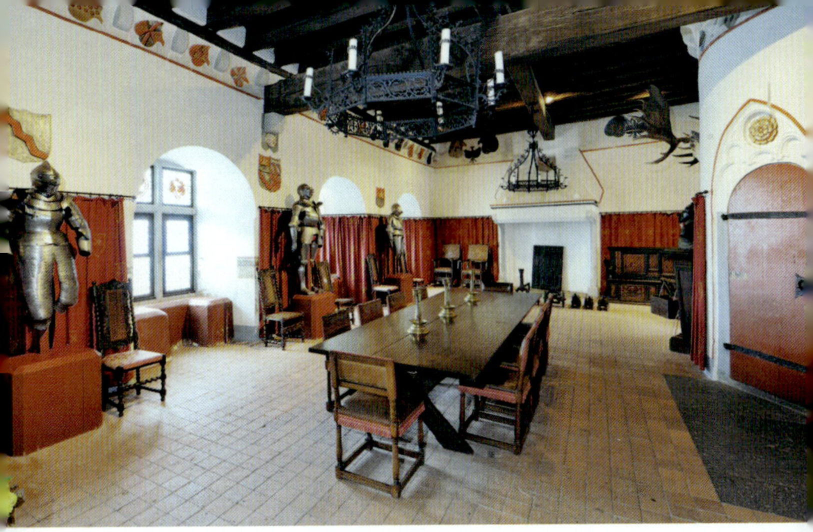

▲ *Knight's hall*

beamed ceilings with clay and then to whitewash them. The **furniture**: a bridal bed, pine wood, painted, Franconia around 1525; five children's portraits, 18th century. – The wall niches contain a collection of 16th to 18th century **ceramics**. The tankards and jugs come from the Westerwald, Siegburg, Raeren and Creussen, all centres for the manufacture of household ceramics during that period.

A **spiral staircase** leads to the floor below. Such stairways saved space and were extremely common in castles. The winding turn of the stairs from the right above to the left below had the castle's defender in mind since he carried his weapon in his right hand. The opposite turn, however, was a disadvantage for the aggressor.

Architecturally, the so-called **hall of banners** is the most sumptuous room in the castle. It has a Late Gothic star-ribbed vault. (The ribs are arranged around the boss in the form of a star.) The stone ribbing not only supports the ceiling but is also decorative. This elegant form of vaulting is found only in the noblest living quarters. The **stained glass windows** in the bay show St George and the dragon. St George was

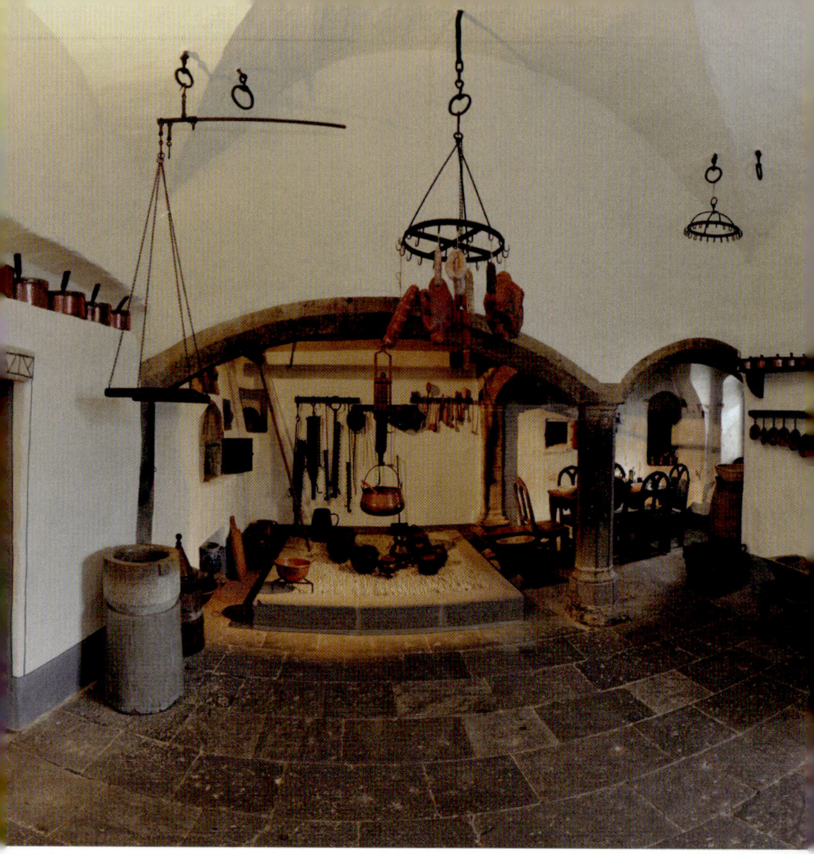

▲ *Rodendorf kitchen*

the patron of all Christian knights. The clock (16th century) and a tiled stove (1871) complete the setting. The tiled stove is a so-called Evangelist's stove (it shows the four Evangelists and family heraldry). It was heated from the kitchen next door. The floor of the room is partly mid-13th century and partly late 15th century.

The **kitchen** of the late Middle Ages has retained its original character (1490). The room is purely utilitarian. It provided the food for the

Eltz-Rodendorf family. Copper cauldrons hung on a hook above the open fire. The hook was moved to adjust the height of the pots and, thus, to regulate the heat. The oven is lined with volcanic tuff stone. Burning wood heated this stone so that bread could be baked on it. In the window niche there is a sink, and in front of it an oak chopping block on which meat and game were prepared. The flour chest is a 15th century piece of household furniture. Rings in the vaulting were used for hanging up provisions. The wall cupboard and pantry contain vessels for everyday use. They date from different centuries.

A visit to the castle is a walk through more than 850 years of history and culture of the Rhine and Moselle. Visitors experience the past through immediate contact with buildings and objects that have survived the centuries. In the 19th century, Eltz Castle was frequently the motif of Romantic paintings and attracted such noteworthy visitors as the poet Victor Hugo and the painter William Turner. Today, Eltz Castle has lost none of its attraction. This is proven by the thousands of visitors each year who come to experience the romantic atmosphere of the castle in the woods for themselves.

Treasure Chamber

The extensive collection of art which is on display in the present treasure chamber was opened to the public in 1981. The five rooms on the lowest floors of the Rübenach House, where the collection is exhibited, were originally storerooms. During restoration work from 1975 to 1981, the rooms were preserved and made into a museum. The Late Mediaeval rooms, which all differ architecturally from one another, convey an impression of the organic form of the building which was determined by the rock on which the castle was built. The size and shape of the rooms on the four lowest floors, and the convenient stairways, made this part of the castle ideal for a museum.

The treasure chamber completes and enhances the historical and cultural tour of the castle. All the exhibits belonged to members of the Eltz family and, originally at least, were acquired for actual use. The 500 or so exhibits include gold- and silversmith's work, ivory carvings, coins, medals, jewellery, glass, porcelain, cutlery, textiles, clothing, weapons, armour and sacred objects.

The first room, the great entrance hall, houses costly 17th and 18th century **hunting weapons** and personal items which belonged to the Elector *Phillip Karl zu Eltz* (1665–1743) and other prominent members of the Eltz family. A statue of **Johannes von Nepomuk**, known as the saint of bridges, stands at the front of the room. It was made by *Franz Christoph Mäderl* in Augsburg in 1752. It is repoussé in silver and cast, fully worked and partly gilded. The 1.10-metre figure stands on a black painted and richly ornamented wooden base, 40 cm high, with the donor's coat-of-arms on the front. The statue is a typical example of the handicraft and artistic skills of Augsburg silversmiths in the 18th century. There is a collection of **Höchst porcelain**, 18th century glass and 16th and 18th century **clocks** at the back of the room.

The next room is dominated by a Mediaeval groin vault and a mighty central pillar. It shows items which used to belong to the Eltz family in Vukovar, including 18th century **Viennese porcelain**, **bronze candelabra**, **furnishings** and **crockery**, and two **portraits** of Count Karl zu Eltz (1846–1900) and his wife.

A narrow staircase leads to the armoury with an oak ceiling which is more than 500 years old. The **collection of arms** in this room includes swords and daggers, crossbows and guns. The splendid **armour** next to the passageway was made around 1500. The next vaulted room houses **gold- and silversmith's work** and **ivory carvings**. The candelabra on the left and right next to the stairs were made in Augsburg in 1630. The display case contains an **ornamental bowl** (around 1680), showing Alexander the Great, various **drinking vessels** in the form of mounted figures, a **Flemish miniature** of St George (made of ivory, around 1420), **tankards** and **ornamental beakers** made of ivory and amber with gilded silver fittings. The gilded **mounted figures** represent, among others, Gustav Adolf, the King of Sweden. They are repoussé in silver and cast, and were made in Augsburg around 1650.

Another staircase leads to the lowest vault in the entire castle. **Sacred objects, jewellery** and **curiosities** are exhibited here. The table

Treasure chamber: Diana on a stag, Augsburg around 1600 ▶

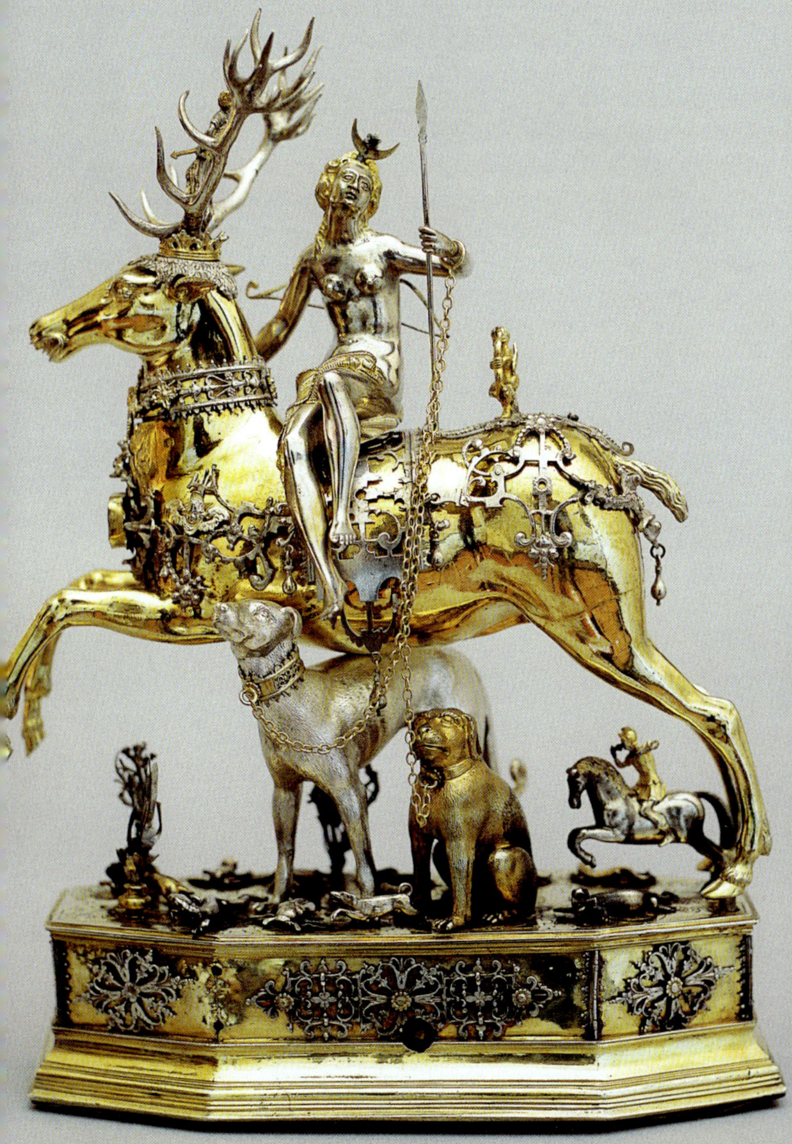

display cases contain jewellery, a richly ornamented Hungarian sword, treasurer' keys, coins and medals. The next display case has three 17th century nefs. The **goddess Diana** on a stag was made in Augsburg around 1600 and was used in a drinking game. She moved, on a base driven by clockwork, along the festively set table. When she stopped, the nearest person had to drink the vessel's entire contents. The **monster**, half dragon and half wild boar, made from a coconut with gold- and silverwork, served as a vessel. The allegorical **»Gluttony conveyed by Drunkenness«**, in the form of a wheelbarrow carrying a fat aristocrat being pushed by Bacchus, is also a vessel. Other items include a Rhenish monstrance (silver, gilded with enamel, 1340), a censer (bronze, 1240), an aspersorium (1150) and other chalices belonging to the Eltz family. The stairs to the exit, three floors up, originally served as a slide for the vats of wine stored in the vaults. The stairs take the visitors back through the 4-metre outer wall of the Rübenach House into the passage to the inner courtyard.

English translation by Dorothy Ann Schade-Maurice, Traunstein
Photographs: Dieter Ritzenhofen, Münstermaifeld. – AV-Studio Wolfgang Kaiser, 56332 Wolken, www.SKYCAM-TV.de: Page 3. – Martin Jermann, F. G. Zeitz KG Königssee: Page 5.
Ground plan: Landesamt für Denkmalpflege Rheinland-Pfalz, Mainz
Printed by F&W Mediencenter, Kienberg

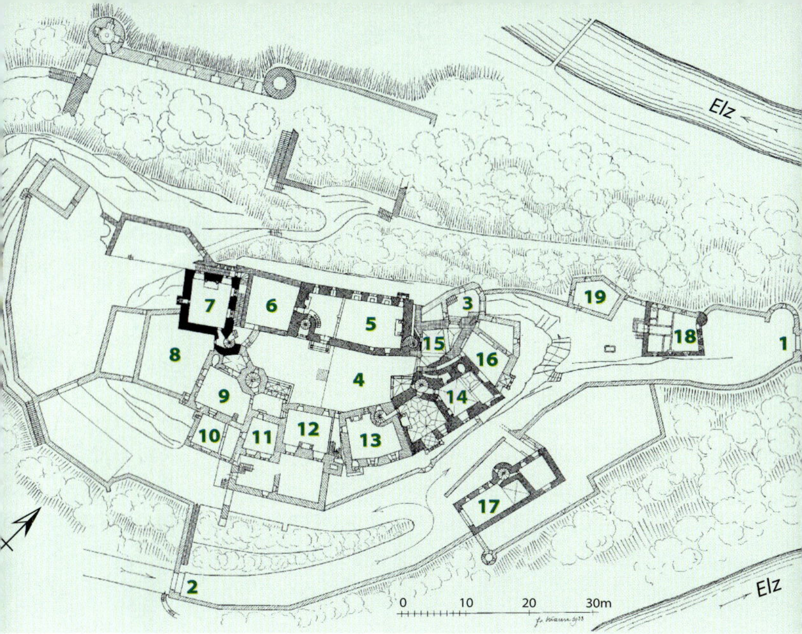

▲ *Ground plan*

1 Outer gateway
2 Valley gate
3 Inner castle gate
4 Inner courtyard
5 Rübenach House
6 Terrace
7 Platt Eltz
8 Castle warden's garden, also known as »Alte Burg«
9 – **12** Kempenich Houses
13 – **15** Rodendorf Houses
16 Chapel
17 Coach house
18 Goldsmith's house
19 Craftsmen's houses

Eltz Castle
Rhineland-Palatinate
Gräflich Eltz'sche Kastellanei Burg Eltz
D-56294 Münstermaifeld
Tel. 02672/95050-0 · Fax 02672/95050-50
www.burg-eltz.de

Eltz castle is open to the public from April 1st to November 1st from 9.30 am to 5.30 pm (beginning of the last guided tour) daily

Front cover: *North side of Eltz Castle*
Back cover: *Treasure chamber: Knight on Horseback, 16th century*

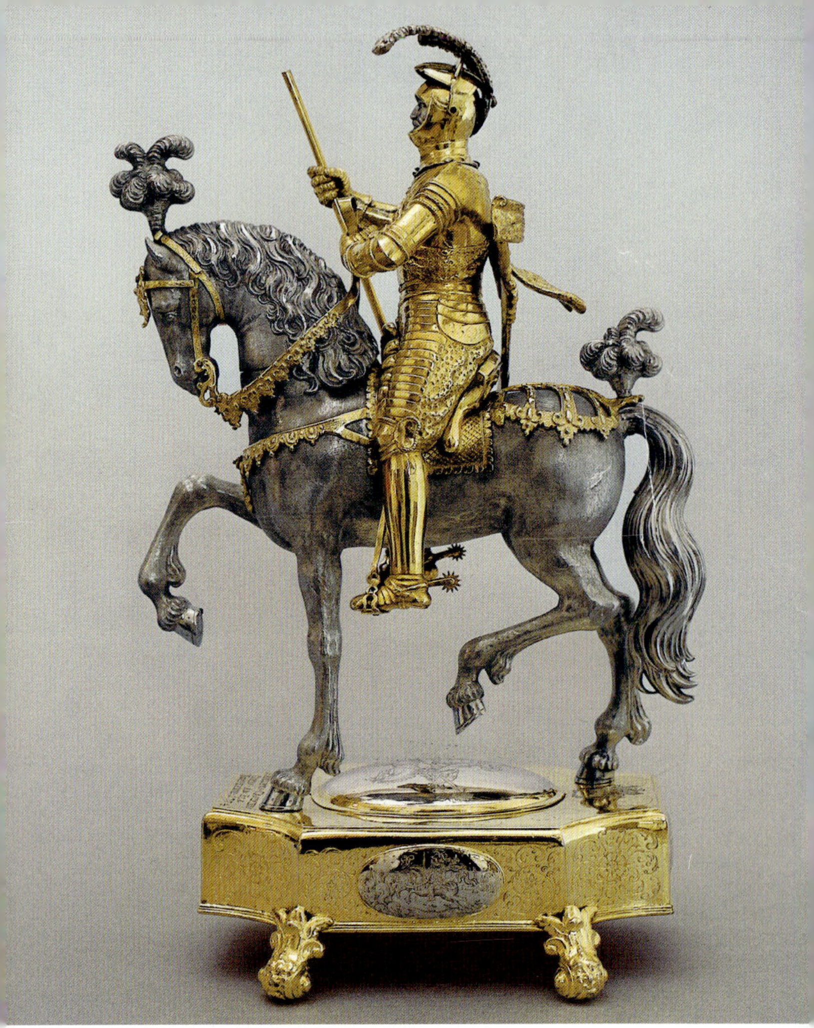

DKV ART GUIDE No. 285
Tenth English edition 2015 · ISBN 978-3-422-02406-9

Paul-Lincke-Ufer 34 · 10999 Berlin
www.deutscherkunstverlag.de